T0268362

IMAGES
of America

NEW YORK'S
WORLD WAR II
AIRCRAFT

Three New York–built aircraft models, along with a pair made in California, made up the backbone of the US Army's fighter forces in World War II. In the foreground is a Bell P-39, built near Buffalo, New York. Next is a North American A-36 Apache, the predecessor to the famous P-51 Mustang. In the center is a Curtiss-Wright P-40, also constructed in Buffalo. Next is a Republic P-47, produced in Farmingdale, New York. Farthest from the camera is a Lockheed P-38 twin-engine fighter. This iconic group was photographed at Wright Field, Ohio, in December 1943. (National Archives, US Army Air Forces.)

ON THE COVER: A Republic P-47 Thunderbolt, fresh from the factory, is inspected by excited New Yorkers during a war bond drive in Manhattan's Financial District in 1944. (National Archives New York City.)

IMAGES
of America

NEW YORK'S
WORLD WAR II
AIRCRAFT

Cory Graff and P.J. Muller

ARCADIA
PUBLISHING

Copyright © 2023 by Cory Graff and P.J. Muller
ISBN 978-1-4671-6035-3

Published by Arcadia Publishing
Charleston, South Carolina

Printed in the United States of America

Library of Congress Control Number: 2023932027

For all general information, please contact Arcadia Publishing:
Telephone 843-853-2070
Fax 843-853-0044
E-mail sales@arcadiapublishing.com
For customer service and orders:
Toll-Free 1-888-313-2665

Visit us on the Internet at www.arcadiapublishing.com

CONTENTS

ACKNOWLEDGMENTS

This book would not have been possible without the generous contributions of many people. The authors would like to thank Janine Kennedy, Holly Reed at the National Archives at College Park, Carey Strumm at National Archives New York City, Mark Stevens, Eric Boehm, Joshua Stoff, Caitrin Cunningham, Helen Thomas at Kennesaw State University Archives and Special Collections, Morrigan Souris, National Archives at Riverside, and Kurt Muller.

Photograph credits are noted in parentheses at the end of each caption. They are as follows: National Archives, Office of War Information (NA/OWI); National Archives, US Army Air Forces (NA/USAAF); National Archives, US Navy (NA/USN); National Archives, US Marine Corps (NA/USMC); Library of Congress (LOC); 7th Fighter Command Association via Mark Stevens (7th FCA); Kennesaw State University Archives and Special Collections (KSU); and Cory Graff (author's collection).

INTRODUCTION

New York state and the history of aviation in the United States have been inseparable since the beginning. Aviation pioneer Glenn H. Curtiss, born in Hammondsport, New York, is often considered more important to the development of aviation than the Wright brothers. Initially tinkering with bicycles and small engines, Curtiss was a motorcycle speed champion by 1903. It was a Curtiss-designed motorcycle engine that powered the first dirigible in the country. His first aircraft design, nicknamed June Bug, flew in New York in 1908; Curtiss himself was the pilot.

Boasting the country's most populous city, along with its location on the western edge of the Atlantic Ocean, made the New York region the heart of flying in the golden age. Curtiss continued to be the individual who often provided the know-how and the nerve. In 1910, the first airplane took off from a ship. It was a Curtiss design. The first practical seaplane was a Curtiss product, too.

When the United States entered World War I, the budding Curtiss Aeroplane and Motor Company transitioned from handcrafting aircraft one at a time to making them by the thousands. The famous JN-4 "Jenny" trainer was the first truly mass-produced plane in American history and was instrumental in teaching famous aviators like Eddie Rickenbacker, Amelia Earhart, and Charles Lindbergh how to fly. In 1919, the Curtiss NC-4 was the first aircraft to cross the Atlantic. Its journey started in New York City. The airfields of New York were often the origin for record-breaking flights. The first aircraft to fly from coast to coast took off from Roosevelt Field in Long Island. More than 26 hours later, the Army Air Service Fokker T-2 landed in San Diego. Lindbergh flew from Roosevelt Field in the other direction. His famous nonstop transatlantic solo flight was made possible by his trusty Ryan NYP, which stood for New York–Paris.

Technology, labor, industry, and knowledge had always converged in New York, so when another war seemed imminent, the region was once again at the vanguard. In a fireside chat on May 26, 1940, Pres. Franklin D. Roosevelt pledged, "We intend to harness the efficient machinery of these manufacturers to the government's program of being able to get 50,000 planes a year." It was a staggering number. That summer, US companies began building combat aircraft at a furious pace. The ever-increasing output bolstered the US military's meager and outdated air assets and also went abroad to help allies already fighting in Europe and Asia.

Curtiss, now known as the Curtiss-Wright Corporation, dusted off the strategies and systems that had generated squadrons of trainers in Buffalo, New York—and at six other manufacturers—years before. This approach, along with planning and procedures developed by the Ford Motor Company to build automobiles, made up the basis for unprecedented aircraft production during World War II. Fighting machines were no longer built in small batches by versatile craftsmen—there was neither time nor enough skilled workers for that. Now, high-volume systems allowed semiskilled workers to each handle a small portion of the overall whole process. As new aircraft moved down the line, one team rattled in a row of rivets, another installed landing gear, and others handled rigging tail surfaces.

With the draft snapping up so many mechanically-minded young males, New York's contemporary pool of workers was immensely diverse. There were old men, young boys and girls, and soldiers awaiting orders to ship overseas. There were more African Americans than ever before, and companies enlisted a massive influx of women. At the height of production in 1944, roughly 40 percent of all aviation workers in New York were female, and they were churning out thousands of brawny and imposing Hellcats, Thunderbolts, and Warhawks.

New York was, in fact, the wartime fighter capital of the free world. Some 62 percent of all single-engine pursuit ships, as the Army Air Forces called them, were from companies headquartered in the Empire State. In the war's darkest days, Buffalo-built Curtiss P-40s went to China to take on the Japanese. Bell P-39s, constructed in nearby Wheatfield, held the tenuous line at New Guinea, Guadalcanal, and the Aleutian Islands. Grumman F4F Wildcats, produced on Long Island, tangled with Zero fighters at Coral Sea and Midway during the first critical carrier battles in the Pacific.

New York's aero companies were prolific wartime exporters. The United Kingdom and France ordered thousands of planes. And when France fell, the American machines went to British and commonwealth service without hesitation. In smaller numbers, New York combat aircraft flew in the world's air forces from Persia and Peru to Portugal and beyond. One of the biggest recipients of Curtiss and Bell aircraft was the Soviet Union. Thousands of New York–built fighters crossed more than half the globe to take on the German Luftwaffe on the eastern front. Warplanes were so undeniably useful that even Axis nations operated some New York aircraft in combat.

At home, not all efforts led to wondrous success. The Bell Aircraft Corporation fought to fit its radical designs into the Army Air Forces' decidedly traditional mindset. Brewster repeatedly failed to live up to the Navy's high standards. And Curtiss, the biggest airplane manufacturer in the state, fought setback after setback, including a never-ending battle to replace its once ubiquitous P-40 Warhawk with something better. On Long Island, Grumman and Republic were seemingly immune to impediments, each making big, brawny machines that were wickedly effective and tough as nails.

After D-Day, German ground troops feared the ever-present "Jabos," a slang term for fighter-bombers. Republic's P-47s roamed overhead like relentless predators, looking for tanks, troops, or trains exposed to assault. A half a world away, Grumman's Hellcats ruthlessly pummeled island bases, shipping, and any Japanese contender that dared come up to intercede. As the US forces closed in on Japan, nearly every aircraft flying from the deck of a US Navy aircraft carrier—whether it was a Hellcat, Helldiver, or Avenger—was conceived on a drawing board in New York. It was the same in the Atlantic, where Grumman-designed Wildcats and Avengers screened massive convoys, always vigilant for the shadow of a U-boat below the surface.

In all, from January 1940 to August 1945, the five New York aviation companies profiled in this volume built 79,170 fighting aircraft, which made up over 26 percent of the country's entire output. That pace amounts to workers producing more than 38 aircraft every single day—or roughly one combat machine every 37 minutes.

One

BELL AIRCRAFT
CORPORATION

When the Consolidated Aircraft Corporation pulled up stakes and left for San Diego in 1935, Bell Aircraft moved into the company's abandoned facility in Wheatfield, located near Buffalo, New York. The company's founder, Lawrence "Larry" Bell, had worked as a manager for Consolidated Aircraft and the Glenn L. Martin Company before setting out on his own.

Bell had a knack for creating unconventional aircraft. His first was a five-man "bomber destroyer." The YFM-1 Airacuda was a peculiar and futuristic-looking plane bristling with guns and powered by two rear-facing Allison engines. But the revolutionary new machine was plagued with problems.

The P-39 Airacobra was similarly strange, with a single engine located in the middle of its fuselage and a propeller driven by a long shaft. The plane was the first fighter to have tricycle landing gear and packed a heavy 37-mm cannon in its nose. The P-39 was one of the standard US Army fighters at the beginning of World War II. While it was unsuited for high-altitude operations, the type served in the Pacific and as a ground-support aircraft for Allied nations, most notably the Soviet Union. A bigger, more powerful version of the P-39, the P-63 Kingcobra, first flew in the last days of 1942. While the P-63 was not used in combat by the United States, a great number were transferred to the Soviet Union. More than 70 percent of the 3,270 P-63s built at Bell went to fight in Russia.

Ever pushing forward, Bell created the country's first jet-powered fighter in 1942. The P-59 Airacomet incorporated a pair of General Electric turbojets, with each one generating 2,000 pounds of thrust. Passed over in favor of more advanced Lockheed designs, some 63 examples were built before the program was completed in mid-1945.

Bell also won the contract to create an experimental high-speed rocket plane in the last months of World War II. Later designated the Bell X-1, the plane would fly to fame in 1947 as the first aircraft recognized to break the sound barrier.

Beyond New York, Bell operated another plant in Marietta, Georgia, that produced more than 600 Boeing-designed B-29 Superfortress bombers under license, the first of which was accepted by the US Army Air Forces in November 1943.

Bell built 13,575 planes from January 1940 to August 1945, representing 4.5 percent of the country's total output. At the height of employment, Bell had about 55,000 men and women on its staff at the factories in New York and Georgia.

Bell's first aircraft, the YFM-1 Airacuda, had pods in front of the engines that held gunners armed with 37-mm cannon designed to blast bombers from the skies. First flown in 1937, the strange machine suffered from poor engine cooling, slow top speeds, and obvious dangers should the gunners have to bail out. Only 13 were made before the Army pulled the plug. However, the peculiar machine put the upstart aircraft producer on the map and compelled the Army to consider other offbeat designs. (NA/USAAF.)

The prototype Airacobra first took to the skies in 1938. In order to improve high-altitude performance, the aircraft was later fitted with a turbosupercharger with a scoop affixed to the left side of its fuselage. The little fighter was revolutionary, with tricycle landing gear and an Allison V-1710 engine situated aft of the pilot. Engine power was provided to the propeller via a long shaft that passed under the cockpit floor. The unusual positioning of the power plant left room for heavy weaponry in later models. (NA/USAAF.)

At Niagara Falls International Airport in Wheatfield, New York, stands the Bell aircraft factory. On a warm evening, the well-lit and expansive floor is populated with dozens of Airacobras just days away from their first flights. The facility boasted more than a million square feet. (LOC.)

A line of P-39s slowly takes shape on Bell's assembly line. These are the fuselages at station 53A. The workers and their tools stayed in one place as ever-growing aircraft components cycled through on wheeled dollies. Elsewhere in the facility, wings, tail assemblies, weaponry, and engines move through similar lines before being joined together at final assembly. (LOC.)

At one of the last stops on Bell's production line, new fighters are filled with fuel and oil. Here, a worker uses a stethoscope to listen for leaks in the fuel tanks in the wing of a P-39 Airacobra. If everything is normal, the next step is to roll the plane outside to the airfield for flight testing. (NA/OWI.)

Loaded down with a pair of .30-caliber machine guns in each wing and two .50-caliber guns in the nose, the P-39D packed a punch—most notably, a hefty 37-mm M4 autocannon that fired down the centerline of the fighter, spitting out 1.3-pound explosive projectiles at 2,000 feet per second. Also shown in this graphic is the long shaft transferring power from the Allison engine to a complex gearbox near the nose and then to the Airacobra's whirling propeller. (NA/USAAF.)

The Royal Air Force considered acquiring Bell's fighter in large numbers. The export version, designated P-400, was equipped with a centerline 20-mm cannon in the place of the 37-mm one installed in American P-39s. This image shows a line of No. 601 Squadron's machines, originally nicknamed Caribous, at Duxford on October 17, 1941. The unit flew only a handful of combat missions before transitioning to Spitfires. (NA/USAAF.)

Aviators in the Pacific often complained that they had to hold the line with older and less effective combat aircraft while the new fighters went to Europe. Here, a P-39D, nicknamed Shrimp and assigned to the 318th Fighter Group, undergoes a change of spark plugs during a 25-hour inspection at Haleiwa, Oahu, Hawaii Territory, on February 15, 1944. The location of the Allison engine made maintenance slightly easier. The closest mechanic is so sure of his footing that he is working in what appears to be loafers. (NA/USAAF.)

Amid a jumble of support equipment, a P-39Q of the 15th Fighter Squadron undergoes maintenance at Haleiwa Field, Hawaii Territory. This aircraft was literally catapulted into combat service off the flight deck of the USS *Nassau* (CVE-16) in late 1943, destined for Canton Island and, later, Makin Atoll in the Gilbert Islands. (NA/USAAF.)

Army ground crews modified a handful of single-place P-39s for training roles. With all of the weaponry removed, there was enough room to extend the cockpit and install dual flight controls. Here, a veteran flyer could teach a student pilot the particulars of operating this unusual fighter. In the best of times, pilots thought the Airacuda was tricky to recover from a spin. The added side surface area of the elongated cockpit required a filet in front of the vertical fin and a strake under the tail to keep the machine controllable. The modified aircraft, redesignated TP-39 (with a T for trainer), inspired a cartoon insignia with a stylized arrow and teepee. (Both, NA/USAAF.)

At Wright Field in Ohio, Army Air Forces evaluators test the guns of a Bell P-39 in a live-fire event. The speeding projectiles are deflected and then trapped in the concrete structure at the far end of the range, while tall berms keep any errant fragments or ricochets from striking the surrounding buildings, aircraft, or people. (NA/USAAF.)

Pilots were wary of the Bell P-39's unusual mid-engine placement. A dark-spirited poem about the Airacobra said it would "tumble and roll" and then "dig a big hole" if the plane entered a spin. This P-39D buried itself in the ground 15 miles from Paine Field in Washington State, seemingly after plummeting nearly straight down, on October 24, 1942. (NA/USAAF.)

The sleek shape of the Airacobra made it an ideal image to be stylized and glorified. This US Army Recruiting Publicity Bureau poster hit the streets in 1943. In reality, P-39s rarely tangled with top-of-the-line German fighters, at least not in the hands of American pilots. The Soviets, however, relied on the aircraft much more heavily in encounters with German invaders on the eastern front. (NA/OWI.)

Soviet ground crewmen rearm a lend-lease P-39 somewhere along the eastern front in 1944. While the reception for the Airacobra was mixed among US Army pilots, the Soviets adored the fighters, using them close to the ground and employing its powerful 37-mm cannon to stop German tanks. They often called the aircraft *Kobruksha*, or "Little Cobra." (NA/USAAF.)

A Soviet fighter pilot poses with the "working end" of his trusty Bell P-39. By way of Iran or Alaska, along with some supplied by Britain, over 4,700 of the fighters flew with the Red Air Force during World War II. Though they were often used for close air support, four of the Soviet Union's top six fighter aces attained a majority of their air-to-air victories in the Airacobra. (NA/USAAF.)

An American Air Transport Command pilot hands over the keys of a Bell P-39 to his Soviet counterpart, most likely near Fairbanks, Alaska Territory. Originally, US pilots would fly the machines into Siberia, but Joseph Stalin objected to US military forces in Russia, so the handoff point was switched to central Alaska. Soviet pilots would stop in Nome for fuel and then continue west. (NA/USAAF.)

At Ladd Field, near Fairbanks, an American soldier changes the owner of a P-39 fighter with a spray gun in 1942. Sporting red Soviet stars, the Airacobra will enter the expansive Soviet Union via Siberia, crossing much of the vast nation to enter the fight against the Germans. Almost 15,000 aircraft built in the United States went to the Soviets under the lend-lease program. (NA/USAAF.)

Many aspects of the Airacobra were unusual, including the cockpit, which was fitted with a set of automobile-style doors complete with roll-down windows. During a high-speed bailout, wind resistance would keep the doors closed, so pilots had to pull a lever on the door that would release it from the fuselage. With a gentle shove, the door flew off. Flyers most often preferred the right side in an emergency because of the protruding throttle quadrant on the left. (NA/USAAF.)

Fuel seeps from the ruptured belly tank of a lend-lease Bell P-39Q in 1943 or 1944. On its way to help with the Soviet war effort, the fighter had an unexpected delay in Alaska after a landing gear failure. The fighter's cumbersome external fuel tank allowed the Airacobra the range to overfly vast areas of the uninhabited north and make the nerve-wracking transit over the Bering Sea to enter Russian airspace. A typed caption affixed to the photograph states, "Flying is precarious around Nome and things like this are bound to happen." (NA/USAAF.)

A P-39D pilot from the 31st Pursuit Group prepares to take to the inky skies over Michigan during war games in 1941. At the time, the unit insignia showed a cobra looking down through the clouds ready to strike. Months later, the unit, redesignated the 31st Fighter Group, exchanged its Airacobras for another New York–made fighter, flying Curtiss P-40s in North Africa. (NA/USAAF.)

At the corner of Old Falls and First Streets in downtown Niagara Falls, New York, a large sign entices would-be war workers to join the growing factory labor force in May 1943. Some of the biggest employers in the area were Bell Aircraft Corporation in Wheatfield and Curtiss-Wright in Buffalo. In many ways, women were more desirable than men for many aircraft-building jobs, as there was no risk they would be drafted. (LOC.)

Office of War Information photographer Marjory Collins captured this picture of a new Bell employee sitting for an identification card image in May 1943. Though it was her first day at the aircraft plant, 45-year-old Mabel Goodwin, a mother of two, was no stranger to factory work—she was part of the labor force in New York during the previous war. (LOC.)

The Airabonita was developed in parallel with the P-39 Airacobra. Built to compete for a spot aboard Navy carriers, the fighter, designated XFL, had a tailhook and tail wheel undercarriage for landing on the deck of a ship. The Bell product was no match for the bigger and faster Corsair design submitted by Connecticut-based Chance Vought. After testing, the sole Airabonita was abandoned at a Navy base and eventually dumped in a landfill. (NA/USAAF.)

What is better than an Airacobra? A Kingcobra. The improved fighter incorporated fixes for many of the P-39's shortcomings. The new P-63 was larger, had a redesigned wing, and had better performance characteristics at high altitude. Despite the Kingcobra being better than the Airacobra in nearly every way, the US Army was committed to superior fighters like the North American P-51 Mustang and Republic P-47 Thunderbolt. More than 70 percent of the 3,303 P-63s produced by Bell went to the Soviet Union. (NA/USAAF.)

Relegated to duties other than frontline combat, several Kingcobras became live training aids for Army aerial gunners. Nicknamed Pinball aircraft, these RP-63s were stripped of their weaponry and standard armor and then reinforced with more than a ton of sheet metal. Gunnery trainees would fire on the planes using frangible bullets designed to disintegrate on impact. Lights in the nose, top, and sides of the fighter would illuminate—like a pinball machine—when the gunner struck home. This 1945 image shows two live-fire targets, Pin Ball and Frangible Sal, along with their brave pilots. (NA/USAAF.)

In this promotional image, two P-63 Kingcobra fighters cruise over Niagara Falls not far from where the planes were built. The aircraft shown fly with Soviet markings and will soon make a very long journey to the war zone. The falls were often used as a dramatic background for photographs of new and notable Bell aircraft. (NA/USAAF.)

A trick often used by the publicity department involved shooting long exposures of aircraft firmly on the ground during live-fire events. With a bit of manipulation, the person who developed the photograph could tilt the frame and blot out any indication of the landing gear, producing a dramatic image that appeared to show the fighter in flight. Here, a P-63 lights up the night skies with six .50-caliber machine guns in the wings and nose with the 37-mm cannon in the center of the propeller spinner likewise spitting fire and lead. (NA/USAAF.)

The availability of Kingcobra airframes coupled with no need to rush them into combat allowed a few aircraft to become test beds for new technologies. Technicians mated two P-63 fuselages to new sets of dramatically swept wings for a Navy experiment. This P-63A was fitted with a V-tail with ruddervators. Famous test pilot Tex Johnston, after nearly spinning the plane into the ground, told the project engineers, "Back to the drawing board, boys." (NA/USAAF.)

High over New York, America's first jet fighter, the Bell P-59 Airacomet, is in the foreground in this formation with Bell Aircraft Corporation's other combat machines. The aircraft in the middle is the P-63 Kingcobra. Bringing up the rear is the P-39, touted in promotional materials as the "first cannon-carrying fighter." The Airacomet shown here is the first of 20 P-59 A-models photographed for advertising on February 14, 1945. (NA/USAAF.)

One of 13 Bell YP-59A Airacomets wheels into a turn high above Rogers Dry Lake in California in 1943. Based at Muroc Army Airfield, examples of the top secret jet were extensively evaluated far from prying eyes. The pioneering jet fighter design had plenty of problems but helped familiarize the Army with new technologies. Once again, Bell Aircraft was first with a revolutionary flying machine. (NA/USAAF.)

With a low rumble instead of the familiar purr of propeller blades, an Airacomet comes to life for a flight at dawn. A ground crewman closes the canopy and will soon climb down, being careful to avoid the engine intakes, which are feeding air to the General Electric turbojets at high velocity. This image shows the pair of bulges in the P-59's belly, which hold the fighter's twin power plants. (NA/USAAF.)

In order for the layman to understand the fundamentals of a jet engine, an artist has superimposed the basics over an image of a P-59. Air comes through the twin intakes (A) and is compressed (B). A mixture of fuel and air is burned (C), and the hot gasses pass through a turbine (D). Near the exhaust, a narrow nozzle (E) increases the gas's velocity. The escaping gasses produce thrust—and a fair amount of noise, too. (NA/USAAF.)

Beyond New York, the Bell Aircraft Corporation made more than just fighter aircraft. Opening a plant in Marietta, Georgia, the company built over 660 Boeing-designed B-29 Superfortress bombers, which were pivotal to the war effort in the Pacific. The Bell Bomber plant employed over 28,000 people, of whom 37 percent were women. It was estimated that 90 percent of the plant's workforce was from the American South. (KSU.)

With a nearly finished B-29 Superfortress as a backdrop, comedian and entertainer Bob Hope and his USO troupe put on a show for the Marietta masses on November 28, 1944. While there was an urgent need for the heavy bombers in combat, periodic breaks in the form of rallies, sports, and shows helped keep morale high and, ultimately, contributed to assure the production lines kept moving. (KSU.)

Most fighter aircraft were big, complex, and expensive. At the dawn of war, the Army requested a tiny interceptor from Bell. The catch, though, was to make it from materials non-vital to the war effort. The XP-77 was wood, not aluminum, and weighed nearly two tons less than an Airacobra. Powered by a Ranger V-12 engine, the mini-fighter would be armed with two machine guns and a 20-mm cannon. Bell's experiment never lived up to its promised performance, and only two were built. (NA/USAAF.)

Weighing as much as nearly five XP-77s, the XP-83 jet-powered escort fighter was touted as a bigger and better Airacomet. Two General Electric J33s hefted the pilot, ample fuel, and six machine guns clustered in the nose. By the time the prototype took to the skies in February 1945, a competing manufacturer had a more promising design. One XP-83 was lost in a crash, and another was scrapped after the war. (NA/USAAF.)

When the Army wanted revolutionary aircraft, they often turned to Bell. The idea of a supersonic research plane was conceived in 1944 and became reality in secret at the Tri-Main building in Buffalo the following year. The rocket-powered craft was originally designated XS-1, for "Experimental, Supersonic." The first powered flight of the craft, now named X-1, took place on December 9, 1946, over the California desert. Bell's designers modeled the X-1 on the shape of a .50-caliber bullet, which was known to be stable at supersonic speeds. Though the X-1 was created during wartime, the innovative plane did not break the sound barrier until October 14, 1947, with World War II fighter ace and Air Force test pilot Capt. Charles "Chuck" Yeager at the controls. (Both, NA/USAAF.)

Two

BREWSTER AERONAUTICAL CORPORATION

Brewster's ambitious advertising tagline during World War II was "For Lasting Mastery of the Air." But as one modern writer put it, the company made "flying junk." Connecticut-based Brewster Carriage Company was making some of the country's finest horse-drawn transportation starting in 1810. The company moved to New York City by 1827 and began constructing automobile bodies in 1907. Work on airplanes came in 1920, when the company signed on to make components for naval aircraft.

In 1932, Brewster & Company's airplane division was purchased by engineer James Work for $30,000. The newly named Brewster Aeronautical Company set up shop in Long Island City and aspired to design entire military aircraft. Its first creation was the Brewster SBA scout and torpedo bomber. The US Navy, concerned that Brewster might be too small and inexperienced to skillfully make planes, awarded the production contract to the Naval Aircraft Factory.

Brewster's first in-house creation was its most infamous. In 1939, the pudgy F2A Buffalo became the Navy's first monoplane fighter, but in combat, it was no match for Japan's nimble Mitsubishi Zero. As one Marine Corps pilot grimly reported, "Any commander who orders pilots out for combat in an F2A should consider the pilot lost before leaving the ground." Buffalos were retired from frontline service after the Battle of Midway. Other nations had much more combat success with the type, most notably Finland, which had acquired 44 of the aircraft (export Model 239s).

Brewster's improved Navy bomber, the SB2A Buccaneer, first flew in 1941. Over time, it seemed that the Navy might have been right to be wary of Brewster and its management. Painful delays and labor disputes slowed delivery of aircraft, and those that did make it to the fleet were often poorly made.

Eventually, Brewster was enticed to construct an established fighter under license. Within the company, the Chance Vought–designed F3A Corsair was called the Brewster Battler. The company's missed deadlines and shoddy workmanship continued even when the Navy briefly took control to "clean house." When the Navy canceled the F3A contract in mid-1944, the company quickly died.

Brewster built 1,927 planes from January 1940 to July 1944, representing just 0.6 percent of the country's total output. At the height of employment, Brewster had about 12,000 men and women on its staff at factories in New York, New Jersey, and Pennsylvania.

Brewster's first aircraft design showed promise in 1936, but the Navy was unsure whether the fledgling company could deliver. As a result, only one aircraft was made at Long Island before the Naval Aircraft Factory in Philadelphia took over the job. Thus, the prototype Brewster SBA scout bomber made way for the SBN. This image shows one of the 30 built in Pennsylvania. The aircraft, already outdated, were retired in the summer of 1942. (NA/USAAF.)

Part of the reason the SBA went nowhere was because the little Brewster fighter seemed more important. In a Navy design competition, the barrel-shaped machine beat out submissions by Seversky and Grumman. The F2A Buffalo became the Navy's first monoplane fighter when it entered service in 1939. Pictured here is the XF2A-1 prototype aloft on a test flight. (NA/USAAF.)

Brewster' XF2A-1 Buffalo fighter is prepared for drag testing at the National Advisory Committee for Aeronautics (NACA) wind tunnel at Langley Research Center in Virginia. The full-scale tunnel cost $900,000—it was completed in 1931 and could simulate speeds up to 120 miles per hour. This picture was taken on May 2, 1938. (LOC.)

Hidden among the trees in a camouflaged revetment at Ewa Marine Corps Air Station on the island of Oahu, Hawaii Territory, crewmen top off the fuel tanks of a Brewster F2A-3 on May 1, 1942. The aircraft was most likely assigned to Marine Fighting Squadron 212 (VMF-212), nicknamed the Hell Hounds.≠ (NA/USN.)

Precariously hanging on to the catwalk of the escort carrier USS *Long Island* (AVG-1), this Brewster F2A-3 Buffalo suffered a landing gear failure when it touched down for landing on July 25, 1942. The fighter's propeller and Curtiss-Wright-made R-1820 Cyclone engine are nearly a complete loss, but the crew is working quickly to safely extract the pilot and then drag the airframe back on to the flight deck. The accident happened off Palmyra Island in the central Pacific Ocean while the fighter was flying with Marine Fighting Squadron 211 (VMF-211), which was the last Navy or Marine Corps unit to operate the Buffalo in frontline service. (Both, NA/USN.)

Other nations flew the Buffalo in combat with varying degrees of success. Here, Royal Air Force "pursuit ships" are assembled after transit to Singapore in 1941 or 1942. While British pilots and their Australian and Kiwi counterparts were highly critical of the fighters, Finnish aviators operated export versions of the Brewster against Soviet air forces to great effect through 1945. They called the fighters "pearls of the northern sky." (LOC.)

Brewster built more SB2A Buccaneers than Buffaloes during the war. The airframe owed much to the earlier SBA design but has a bigger engine and more expansive dimensions. However, the SB2A Buccaneer scout bomber was a failure in the eyes of the US Navy and Royal Air Force. It was poorly constructed and still underpowered, making it not suitable for combat. All orders were canceled in 1943. (NA/USN.)

Outside Brewster's factory in Johnsville, Pennsylvania, models perched on the wings give an idea of the sheer size of a Buccaneer during a promotional photograph shoot in July 1943. The big aircraft weighed nearly five tons empty and could heft two more tons in the form of fuel, ammunition, depth charges, or bombs. (NA/OWI.)

Before the military buys an aircraft, manufacturers often make a full-scale mock-up. This image shows Brewster's attack aircraft hopeful, made mostly of wood, on May 9, 1942. When the real prototype XA-32 aircraft took to the skies for the first time more than a year later, it did so with a heavily revised tail layout. (NA/USAAF.)

Seen on a test flight in July 1943 is Brewster's behemoth, the XA-32. This version was powered by an R-2800 radial engine with plans for an upgrade to a bigger R-4360 at a later date. The wings were loaded to the gills with weaponry, eight .50-caliber machine guns, and four 37-mm autocannon. Missed deadlines and poor performance doomed the project. Only two examples were built. (NA/USAAF.)

When Brewster failed at building its own designs, the Navy worked to give the company the task of manufacturing aircraft under license. Chance Vought's F4U Corsair fighter was badly needed for action in the Pacific. Brewster's version, designated F3A-1, was a poor copy never trusted to serve in combat. Most of the 735 planes produced were used only for stateside training. (NA/USN.)

The Industrial Incentive Division of the Navy worked to reinforce the importance of the bent-wing Corsair with posters like this one. The original designer, Chance Vought, built them in Stratford, Connecticut. Goodyear Aircraft made more in Akron, Ohio. Brewster's facility in Long Island City pitched in with more. When Brewster's contracts were canceled, some of the partly completed airframes were moved to Goodyear for completion. (NA/OWI.)

Three

CURTISS-WRIGHT
CORPORATION

Buffalo-based aviation behemoth Curtiss-Wright had three divisions: airframes, engines, and propellers. During World War II, the company became one of the biggest contractors and employers in the United States.

The company's core wartime product was the venerable Curtiss P-40 Tomahawk/Warhawk Army fighter. From the moment the United States entered World War II, P-40s were in action, fighting Japanese aircraft over Pearl Harbor and Clark Field in the Philippines on December 7 and 8, 1941. Even before, P-40s were serving in combat in North Africa with the British Royal Air Force and in China with the American Volunteer Group, better known as the Flying Tigers.

While the P-40 was somewhat less modern than other contemporary fighter designs, Curtiss could make its fighter quickly and in staggering numbers. Some 13,700 P-40s were built until the end of 1944, and they served with a multitude of Allied nations, from the frozen Russian tundra to the jungles of New Guinea.

Curtiss also contributed a massive cargo plane to the war effort. The C-46 Commando was nearly twice as big as its counterpart, the Douglas C-47 Skytrain. Heavily loaded with fuel, food, and supplies, Army C-46 Commandos regularly crossed the Himalayan Mountains from India to supply Allied troops in China.

In the Pacific, the Curtiss SB2C Helldiver replaced the beloved Douglas Dauntless on US Navy carriers in 1944 and 1945. The Curtiss plane was bigger and faster than its predecessor but never as well-liked.

In fact, there were difficulties with many Curtiss products manufactured during the war. Helldivers had stability and control problems, Commandos were rumored to sometimes burn or explode, and Curtiss was never able to completely modernize its staple P-40 fighter. Beyond, flyers often looked at Curtiss propellers with suspicion, and defective Wright engines were delivered to the Army. Many believe that these wartime issues caused the government to lose faith in the company, and by 1948, Curtiss-Wright's Airplane Division was dissolved.

Curtiss built 26,637 planes from January 1940 to August 1945, representing 8.8 percent of the country's total wartime output. The company also made more than 142,000 engines and 146,000 propellers. At the height of employment, Curtiss had about 180,000 men and women on its staff at factories in New York, Ohio, Missouri, and Kentucky.

Dutifully wearing his wartime guest pass, New York governor Thomas Dewey (left) tours the Buffalo Curtiss-Wright Corporation Airplane Division plant on August 23, 1943. At the time, the company was the nation's second-largest employer (behind General Motors). Some 43,000 Curtiss employees worked at Buffalo, "the largest combat plane plant in the nation," according to the *Encyclopedia of New York State* in 2005. (NA/OWI.)

With a bang from a black powder charge, a Curtiss SOC Seagull floatplane launches from the port catapult of a New Orleans Class heavy cruiser in 1942 or 1943. The aircraft worked as the eyes for the vessel's main guns. Upon return, the airplane landed in the smooth water left by the ship's wake and was hoisted aboard by crane. Slowly replaced by more modern scout planes, SOCs stayed in Navy service until the end of World War II. (NA/USN.)

The Curtiss P-36 Hawk was one of the Army's primary fighters before World War II. This aircraft, a P-36C, was assigned to the 1st Pursuit Group in 1939. The fighter's temporary, unofficial camouflage paint scheme was applied for exhibition at the National Air Races in Cleveland and, later, war games at Maxwell Field in Alabama. (NA/USAAF.)

A derivative of the P-36, the YP-37 flew with a 1,000-horsepower Allison V-12 engine. The cockpit was moved dramatically aft to make room for an expansive turbosupercharger. Pilots complained they could not see a thing on takeoff or landing. The project was canceled in favor of another, more conventional Curtiss fighter design. Only 14 YP-37s were made. (NA/USAAF.)

Army officials used two YP-37s, assigned to the 8th Pursuit Group in Langley, Virginia, to experiment with cold-weather flying in the Alaska Territory in 1940. It was not encouraging that ground crews painted bright orange accents on the planes' noses, tails, and wings, making them easier to spot if they went down in the snow. Here, one of the Curtiss fighters is shown fitted with a set of skis in place of its customary tires and wheels. (NA/USAAF.)

The Curtiss P-40 Warhawk was the Army's primary fighter aircraft at the dawn of World War II. This P-40B was photographed less than two months before the attack on Pearl Harbor. Sleek, tough, and fast, the Warhawk had a leg up on the competition, because much of its airframe was similar to the previous P-36 Hawk. More than 13,700 P-40s were built—all in Buffalo, New York. (NA/USAAF.)

The major upgrade from the P-36 to the P-40 was its engine. Warhawks flew with a liquid-cooled Allison V-1710 that generated over 1,000 horsepower. This aircraft was most likely assigned to the 8th Pursuit Group, based at Mitchell Field, New York, in 1941. (NA/USAAF.)

With the engine roaring at flying attitude, Royal Air Force fitters run a test on the engine of Curtiss Tomahawk Mark IIB at the No. 107 Maintenance Unit in Kasfareet, Egypt. Note the two unlucky crewmen putting their weight on the bar inserted in the tail of the fighter to assure that the aircraft does not tip forward and crunch its propeller and engine. (NA/USAAF.)

Aviators of the Royal Air Force were the first to paint the iconic shark mouth on the nose of the Curtiss P-40s. American Volunteer Group pilots saw this photograph on the cover of a magazine and copied the motif. The Mark IIB Tomahawk in the foreground was assigned to No. 112 Squadron in Egypt. Flying officer Neville Bowker's fighter, nicknamed Menace, is pictured here in the fall of 1941. (NA/USAAF.)

Known as the Flying Tigers, the pilots of the American Volunteer Group gave up their commissions in the US military to fight the Japanese in China. One hundred P-40s slated for Britain were diverted to the three squadrons. This image shows members of the 3rd Squadron, known as Hell's Angels, on May 28, 1942, near the Salween River Gorge. (NA/USAAF.)

This unique view of an early-model Curtiss P-40B during maintenance reveals its "long-nose" Allison engine with an extended propeller shaft for maximum streamlining. Below it are a trio of cylindrical radiators for oil and Prestone coolant. In this image, a mechanic, a long way from his home in Boise, helps with an overhaul in Kunming, China, on September 26, 1942. (NA/USAAF.)

Somewhere in China, an air-raid warning sounds, and American pilots sprint toward their Curtiss P-40 fighters. This scramble took place on November 2, 1943, after the Flying Tigers had been integrated in the US Army Air Forces, becoming the 23rd Fighter Group. They continued to use the Flying Tiger nickname. (NA/USAAF.)

During the attack on Pearl Harbor, air bases on Oahu were pounded by the Japanese. Many P-40s were among the roughly 180 US aircraft destroyed. This image shows one of the Curtiss fighters charred and mangled at Wheeler Field, where the aircraft had been neatly lined up in front of the hangars. The airfield was one of the primary attack points for the first wave of Japanese attack aircraft. Only a handful of American pilots managed to make it into the air that morning. (NA/USAAF.)

The original emblems of the Flying Tigers were created by Walt Disney Studios and applied to the Curtiss fighters as decals. As shown here, after the United States entered the war with Japan, the leaping tiger design was augmented with a patriotic top hat and shredded Japanese flag. It is being applied by Sergeant Larue in February 1943. (NA/USAAF.)

In Iceland, Army recovery crews dismantle a Curtiss-Wright P-40K Warhawk that crash-landed due to engine failure on a farm in the east part of Skorradalur in Borgarbyggð. The crash took place on August 17, 1943. The plane was fully dismantled and hauled away by truck. Pilot John W. Bigelow was unhurt in the accident. (NA/USAAF.)

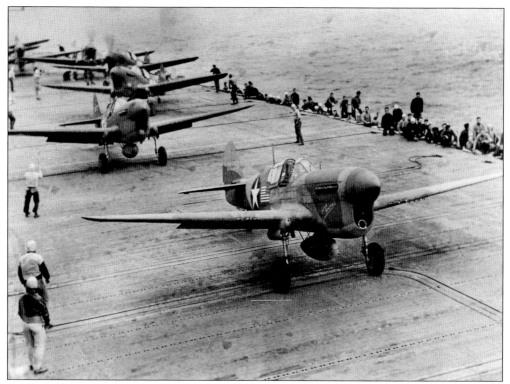

Headed into combat, Army Air Forces P-40F Warhawks prepare for takeoff from the deck of the USS *Chenango* (AVC-28) on November 10, 1942. These aircraft were assigned to the 33rd Fighter Group and slated to be based at a landing strip near Port Lyautey in French Morocco. (NA/USN.)

An Italian news photograph reveals the sad fate of a pair of Curtiss P-40Fs of the 325th Fighter Group, caught at their parking spots in a bombing raid near the Tunisian front. Note the 48-star US flag insignia painted on the underside of the left wing of each thoroughly wrecked aircraft. (Author's collection.)

At an airbase in Casablanca, Morocco, a squadron of Curtiss P-40F Warhawk fighters changes hands in a formal ceremony. On January 9, 1943, the US Army Air Forces 33rd Fighter Group turned over its machines to Free France's Groupe de Chasse 2/5, better known as the Lafayette Escadrille. From this point on, the unit would only fly New York–built aircraft in combat in World War II—P-40s and, later, Republic P-47s. (NA/USAAF.)

A silk-scarfed flier assists the armorers while they are loading .50-caliber ammunition into the guns of his P-40 fighter near Kunming, China. The pilot, photographed here in early 1943, is Robert L. Scott Jr., who later wrote the famous memoir *God Is My Co-Pilot* about his experiences with the Flying Tigers. (NA/USAAF.)

With minimal support equipment but plenty of mud, mechanics of the 51st Fighter Group used empty 55-gallon drums to work on the Allison engine of a Curtiss P-40E. In 1942, the unit was assigned to defend bases in India and China, flying patrol missions and attacking Japanese ground units in support of Chinese army troops in the area. (NA/USAAF.)

Six .50-caliber guns spout lead and flame during a nighttime firing session in Buffalo. Early clashes in Europe pointed to the need for heavier weaponry, with six hard-hitting M2 Browning machine guns being the standard. One of Curtiss-Wright's press photographers captured this weapons synchronization session in March 1942. (NA/USAAF.)

Former University of Oregon track star Robert W. Deiz poses with his Curtiss P-40 Warhawk in the Mediterranean. Deiz was a member of the 332nd Fighter Group, the Tuskegee Airmen, manned almost entirely by African American personnel. He shot down two German Focke-Wulf Fw 190 fighters in two days and flew 93 combat missions during his service in the US Army Air Forces. (NA/USAAF.)

A mechanic of the 99th Fighter Squadron takes a rare moment to relax in the wing of one of the unit's Curtiss fighters. The initial group of the famed Tuskegee Airmen flew its first combat mission in North Africa in June 1943. African American combat pilots went on to down 261 enemy aircraft in combat in World War II. (NA/USAAF.)

Many Curtiss P-40s, often the oldest ones, made their way into the hands of the Soviets via lend-lease arrangements with Great Britain and the United States. Here, a heavily retouched newspaper photograph shows the commander of the 126th Fighter Aviation Regiment, Maj. Viktor Naidenko, briefing a combat mission with his pilots in the winter of 1941. (NA/USAAF.)

The 15,000th Curtiss Hawk fighter built at the Buffalo plant, a P-40N Warhawk, flew for the cameras emblazoned with the insignia of the 28 air forces operating Curtiss fighters during the war. The aircraft, stripped of its celebratory flourishes, was turned over to the US Army Air Forces on November 22, 1944. (NA/USAAF.)

The caption on the back of this image reads, "A busy scene in one of the Curtiss-Wright corporation's plants, showing planes of all kinds, much needed by the Allies. Those in the foreground are Curtiss fighters, while the large planes on the left are 25-ton transport planes." The picture was taken in Buffalo in January 1943, showing production of P-40s and C-46 cargo aircraft. (NA/USAAF.)

At an airfield in China, a Nationalist guard stands watch over a row of American Curtiss P-40 Warhawks. Though it is only 1942, the planes look battered by heavy use, dirt airstrips, and harsh conditions. A close look at the aircraft in the foreground reveals that the engine cowling is borrowed from another aircraft, and the iconic hand-painted shark mouth artwork no longer lines up correctly. (NA/USAAF.)

What is more fun than flying a P-40 fighter? Having a monkey as a friend is pretty good. This picture shows pilot Lt. Marshall Carney of Churchland, Virginia, and his squadron's mascot Josephine. Sadly, Carney was killed in an airplane crash while he was on his way to join the 79th Fighter Group in the Mediterranean on October 20, 1943. (NA/USAAF.)

The streamlined nose and distinctive cooling scoop of the Warhawk seemed the perfect canvas for artistic expression. Here, the pilots of the 343rd Fighter Group play cards in front of their P-40Es based at a remote airfield on Umak Island, Alaska Territory, in 1942. Nicknamed the Aleutian Tigers, these fliers protected the chain of islands stretching across the Pacific toward Japan. (NA/USAAF.)

A death's-head skull adorns the nose of a P-40N parked at Nagaghuli Airfield in India. The aircraft was assigned to the 80th Fighter Group, known as the Burma Banshees. The photograph was most likely taken in December 1943, as the acerbic inscription on the bomb affixed to the Warhawk's belly reads, "Merry Xmas 'Tojo.'" (NA/USAAF.)

A photograph taken in Kunming, China, inadvertently underscores the dangers of combat flying in Asia. The plane in the sky, the 308th Bomb Group's B-24 Liberator (nicknamed Sherazade), was destroyed in a crash on January 25, 1944. The P-40 below it, dubbed the Nipponese Nemesis, was flown by fighter ace Matt "Charlie" Gordon Jr. of the 23rd Fighter Group. He was killed near Kalaikunda, India, just a few days before the end of the war. (NA/USAAF.)

In attempts to stay at the top of the fighter game, Curtiss designers pulled three Curtiss P-40s from the production line to be chopped, supercharged, and updated to make the Army-designated XP-40Q. The Q-models were the best Warhawks ever made but not as good as contemporary P-51 Mustangs. This example survived the war only to catch fire during an air-racing competition. The pilot parachuted to safety. (NA/USAAF.)

While some American fighter aircraft soldiered on after the end of hostilities, most P-40s met an end in a smelter. Stripped of their engines, these Warhawks await their fate at Walnut Ridge in Alabama. There were 462 briefly parked there. To save space, they were stored vertically before ultimately being shredded and melted into ingots. (NA/USAAF.)

An aircraft contemporary to the P-40 worked as a test bed for years. Originally a P-36 airframe, the XP-42 demonstrated solutions to streamlining a radial engine. Powered by an R-1830 Twin Wasp, this iteration of the machine had a tightly cowled power plant with a modest cooling scoop below and a snorkel-like carburetor inlet on top. (NA/USAAF.)

In this image from early 1942, a lineup of Curtiss SO3Cs are ready to take to the skies. The aircraft still retain the national insignia, which includes the red center. Built to replace the Curtiss Seagull biplane, the new scout plane's builder called the machine the Seamew. However, the Navy stubbornly reverted to referring to the SO3C as the Seagull, which caused a fair bit of confusion among aviators. (NA/USAAF.)

In Washington State, a Curtiss SO3C-2 Seamew prepares for flight in December 1943. Wags called the scout plane about as pretty as a mid-air collision. Designed to fly from runways or a ship, the Seamew could be equipped with wheels or a single float. The plane was powered by an equally ugly Ranger V-770 inverted V-12 engine, which generated around 520 horsepower. (NA/USN.)

Originally developed as a fully pressurized airliner in 1937, the Curtiss model CW-20 "Condor III" caught the attention of the US military. The C-46 Commando was never as ubiquitous as the Douglas C-47, but it could carry much more. Originally designed for 36 paying passengers, the military version could heft 40 soldiers and their weaponry, 30 wounded people in stretchers, or 7.5 tons of cargo. (NA/USAAF.)

The sheer size of the Curtiss Commando is apparent in this image as crews work on the airplane's R-2800 Double Wasp engines from tall maintenance stands. The Mountain Goat, a C-46A, was photographed at Karachi Airfield, India, in 1943. (NA/USAAF.)

A 1944 Government Printing Office poster implores home front workers to keep building for the war effort. While this element of war is often overlooked in history books, it takes huge quantities of fuel, food, ammunition, and men to make any army effective. (NA/OWI.)

The Commando's natural environment, it seems, was the foreboding sky over some of the roughest territory on the planet. Pilots called the hazardous route over the Himalayan Mountains the Hump. This loaded C-46A was photographed on February 22, 1945, high above the jagged snowcapped peaks. (NA/USAAF.)

A loaded Douglas C-47 Skytrain rumbles into the skies over a Curtiss C-46 in the process of being readied for a similar cargo run. The perspective is deceptive; the Commando was much bigger and boasted double the cargo space of the Douglas aircraft. On the flip side, the Commando was more complex, more costly, and a newer design, meaning there were many more bugs to work out in the remote China, Burma, India (CBI) theater. (NA/USAAF.)

At the 1338th Army Air Forces Base Unit in Yunnanyi, China, a battered Commando ends its days as a building on the airfield grounds. A wartime newspaper, the *CBI Roundup*, stated, "Once it hurdled the Hump. Now this C-46 transport plane is a coffee shop at an ATC (Air Transport Command) base in China. It crashed into a mountainside, ending its flying days." This photograph was taken in January 1945. (NA/USAAF.)

The Army staged this photograph for the benefit of Wirephoto newsmen to reveal the cargo capacity of a new Curtiss Commando in July 1942. The angled ramp near the cargo door shows how the Jeeps are coaxed up into the expansive cargo hold of the aircraft. With the C-46, boasts the news copy, "six continents and seven oceans" are all within reach. (NA/USAAF.)

Nearly everything used to make war in China came from the belly of a cargo plane—gasoline, rations, bombs, and even mules. Here, a Commando, powered by a pair of Pratt & Whitney R-2800 engines, carries spares in its spacious cargo hold. The 18-cylinder Double Wasp was the heart of some of the most famous fighter aircraft of the war, including the Thunderbolt, Hellcat, and Corsair, but these 2,000-horsepower engines are probably headed into the field to help revive another stranded C-46. (NA/USAAF.)

Somehow simultaneously sleek and yet obsolete at the same time, a Curtiss O-52 Owl scout plane has escaped the Buffalo factory for the skies in 1942. Judged unsuited for modern combat, a few of the 203 built were turned over to the Soviets, who used them near the dangerous front lines. American versions were used for training and antisubmarine patrols and as courier aircraft. (NA/USAAF.)

A design feature of the Owl that was modern by late-1930s standards was its articulating main landing gear. This strange but creative scheme was employed by several different aircraft companies, including Grumman for its Wildcat fighter. While engineers attempted to get the deployed wheels as far apart as possible, pilots often had difficulty safely controlling the aircraft on grass or dirt airfields. (NA/USAAF.)

The first Curtiss Helldiver literally had an up-and-down career. It first flew in December 1940. Less than two months later, it crashed due to engine failure, and the tail was torn off. Using this unfortunate event to their advantage, Curtiss designers created larger tail surfaces for added stability. The aircraft was lost in December 1941 when the tail tore apart during a vertical dive. The pilot parachuted to safety. (NA/USN.)

Nearing the end of the assembly line, another Curtiss SB2C is almost ready for delivery to the Navy. The wings got folded for efficient storage in the taxiway outside. Though they were designed in New York, Helldivers were built at the Curtiss plant in Columbus, Ohio, as well as two factories in Canada. Another version, made at Curtiss St. Louis for the US Army, was designated the A-25A Shrike. (NA/USN.)

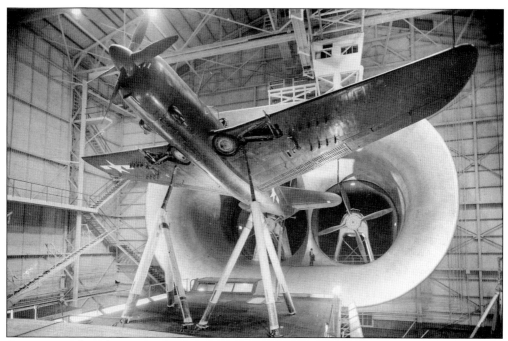

Carrier aircraft in the vast reaches of the Pacific had to fly for hundreds of miles. Here, a Curtiss SB2C-4 is mounted in the National Advisory Committee for Aeronautics (NACA) full-scale wind tunnel for drag cleanup investigation. Aerodynamic specialists tracked down every suspected source of unnecessary drag in order to make the aircraft more efficient. In wartime, a few extra minutes of flight time might mean the difference between success and disaster. (NA/USN.)

A deck crewman aboard the USS *Ticonderoga* (CV-14) strolls past a line of Helldivers in October 1944. Over his shoulder is a belt of 20-mm ammunition used in the pair of AN/M2 wing guns mounted in each of the big bombers. Soon, the aircraft will be involved in strikes on targets in the Philippines. (NA/USN.)

Loaded down with bombs, Curtiss SB2C-4 Helldivers cruise over the US invasion fleet on their way to pound strongpoints on Iwo Jima. The image was captured by a photographer from the USS *Yorktown* (CV-10) on February 22, 1945, just three days after the landings began there. (NA/USN.)

A quick-fingered photographer captured the final moments of a Helldiver near the USS *Lexington* (CV-16). The pilot most likely shoved the throttle forward after getting the wave-off signal from the landing signal officer. As he "poured on the coals," the unchecked torque of the bomber's big Wright R-2600 engine pulled the machine up and over. (NA/USN.)

The crew of a Helldiver poses next to the trusty machine that most fliers called the Beast. The young man on the left is the radioman/gunner, with his hand on the twin .30-caliber mount. The weapon was built into the airframe to keep faster fighters at bay as the SB2C lined up to drop its payload. Separated by quite a distance in the long cockpit, the two men communicated through an intercom system. (NA/USN.)

This is no way to treat a guest. A Helldiver assigned to Bombing Squadron 7 (VB-7) aboard the USS *Hancock* (CV-19) comes to grief on the radio mast of the USS *Intrepid* (CV-11) after a night landing on October 30, 1944. The SB2C-3 may have been diverted because of a fouled deck, battle damage, or low fuel during operations at Leyte Gulf. (NA/USN.)

Between bombing missions, deck crewmen remove the cowling from a Helldiver to work on the Wright R-2600 Double Cyclone engine. Maintenance aboard the carriers often took place under terrible conditions. Mechanics had to contend with a rolling deck, adverse weather, and quick turnaround times. (NA/USN.)

After the cessation of hostilities, a Helldiver assigned to Bombing Squadron 85 (VB-85) aboard the USS *Shangri-La* (CV-38) buzzes low over Omori prison camp near Tokyo. Prisoners, some of whom had been captured in the first days of the war, stand on the rooftops to welcome the aviators. This photograph was taken on or around August 28, 1945. (NA/USN.)

After the war, many nations benefited from surplus American equipment. Here, crewmen load New York–built Curtiss SB2Cs and Grumman F6F Hellcats of the French Fleet Air Arm aboard the *Dixmude*, an escort carrier built in the United States, loaned to the British during the war, and then turned over to the French in April 1945. The vessel and its aircraft were used in combat actions in Indochina in 1947. (NA/USN.)

Slightly smaller than a P-40 but built with the same basic engine, the XP-46A was supposed to iron out all of the Warhawk's shortcomings. However, the improved fighter, which some Curtiss officials likened to the British Supermarine Spitfire, was sluggish enough that the Army canceled the project after just two aircraft were produced. (NA/USAAF.)

The constant struggle to find a successor to the Warhawk was an ugly affair for Curtiss that resulted in some equally hideous aircraft. This endeavor was the XP-60, which flew with numerous engines, airframe modifications, and a multitude of promises to the Army. In the end, the military persuaded Curtiss to make Republic-designed P-47s under license instead of green-lighting this aircraft type. (NA/USAAF.)

Built to behave like a wartime light bomber, the pint-size Curtiss AT-9 Jeep helped student fliers make the leap from single-engine to twin-engine aircraft. With Lycoming radials, retractable landing gear, and an intentionally difficult temperament, the Jeep got prospective pilots ready to handle equally challenging aircraft like the P-38, P-61, and B-26. This aircraft, the first in the production run, was involved in several nonfatal crashes during training duties at Wright Field during the war. (NA/USAAF.)

A group of 24 aviators, two to a plane, pose for a publicity photograph at Ellington Field, Texas. The base had been a flight academy since the United States entered into World War I and served as the training ground for twin-engine transition in the 1940s as the USAAF Advanced Flying School. About 2,800 bomber pilots per year graduated from Ellington, which was about 10 percent of the total who did so during the war years. (NA/USAAF.)

Fearing a shortage of duralumin in wartime, the US military contracted with Curtiss to create a cargo plane from wood. There were high hopes for the project when this artist's rendition was created in 1941. The high-winged, twin-engine aircraft was slated to carry 45 troops or tons of supplies. The first one flew on May 3, 1943. (NA/USAAF.)

Some of the first YC-76 Caravans are pictured on the production line at the Curtiss factory in St. Louis, Missouri, in the last days of 1942. An AT-9 Jeep trainer gives an idea of the scale of the big wooden aircraft, each powered by two R-1830 Twin Wasp radial engines. The cargo plane's weight, which affected its performance, along with no significant shortage of light alloys, quickly doomed the project. Only 25 were produced. (NA/USAAF.)

The wildly unconventional Curtiss XP-55 Ascender was an experiment in improved pilot visibility, armament, and atypical design. An Allison V-1710 engine and pusher propeller propelled the strange aircraft from behind. This airframe, the first of three built, crashed on November 15, 1943. The Curtiss test pilot parachuted to safety, and the Ascender fell 16,000 feet and ended up flattened in a farmer's field. (NA/USAAF.)

In some ways, the XP-55 harkened back to Glenn Curtiss's original aircraft designs, which were pusher planes, with the propeller behind the pilot. Understandably, a safe bail out option was an immediate source of concern among pilots. To make survival a reality, Curtiss designers built the fighter with a lever in the cockpit that would release the entire propeller from the airframe. (NA/USAAF.)

When the long-promised Chrysler IV-2220 inverted V engine did not show, Curtiss engineers slipped a Pratt & Whitney R-2800 in the nose to the XP-60C fighter, causing a 20-percent reduction in horsepower. However, for a moment, it looked like Curtiss had a winner. Further tests revealed that the fighter was slower, heavier, and guzzled more gas than a P-51 Mustang. Curtiss never got the large Army contract it had hoped for. (NA/USAAF.)

Big, speedy, and heavily armed, the Curtiss XP-62's most unique feature was a fully pressurized cockpit. Built to chase high-flying bombers at 37,000 feet, the XP-62 had a 2,300-horsepower Wright Duplex-Cyclone that drove two three-bladed contrarotating propellers. In range of its quarry, the original version of the fighter could let loose with up to eight 20-mm autocannon. Development of the unique aircraft was slow, and the Army pulled the plug on the project in late 1943. (NA/USAAF.)

Designed to be flown from an aircraft carrier, the Curtiss XF14C bucked the trend of naval aircraft with air-cooled power plants. This machine would fly with a Lycoming XH-2470 liquid-cooled, H-configured engine. When progress slowed on the peculiar power plant, Curtiss substituted a Wright R-3350 Duplex-Cyclone. Like the XP-62, the XF14C had a pressurized cockpit. However, development delays killed the project soon after its first flight in July 1944. (NA/USN.)

In 1945, another unusual naval prototype took to the skies. The Curtiss XF15C "Stingeree" straddled the line between the present and future, equipped with an R-2800 radial engine up front and an Allis-Chalmers J36 turbojet behind. Combined, the engines produced a whopping 4,800 horsepower. This image shows the second machine, designated XF15C-1, with a redesigned tail. Only three of the aircraft were built. (NA/USN.)

Created to replace slower and older scout seaplanes, the Curtiss SC Seahawk could fly with a single main float or operate with wheels. The first Seahawks came into Navy service in October 1944, flying from the large cruiser USS *Guam* (CB-2). Although the Seahawk was quite successful, the proliferation of helicopters made these scout aircraft obsolete in the 1950s. Not one Curtiss Seahawk survives today. (NA/USN.)

Late in the war, the soon-to-be-famous battleship USS *Missouri* (BB-63) departs for operations near Japan. On the fantail are a pair of new Curtiss-built SC-1 Seahawk scout planes. The aircraft were used to spot for the ship's massive 16-inch main guns. Only 577 of the aircraft, considered America's best floatplane of the war, were built before hostilities ended in August 1945. (NA/OWI.)

Four

GRUMMAN AIRCRAFT ENGINEERING CORPORATION

Grumman was destined to become the Navy's best contractor. Similar to Brewster, Leroy Grumman's new company started out making airplane parts in 1930 before moving on to design entire aircraft and moving to Bethpage, New York.

Also similar to Brewster, Grumman built a monoplane carrier fighter, the F4F Wildcat, which saw service at the beginning of World War II. While Brewster's Buffalo was soon discarded, the Wildcat soldiered on against superior Japanese aircraft until Grumman could make an even more effective machine.

The F6F Hellcat, dubbed a Wilder Wildcat at Grumman, would be the most successful US fighter of the war, with a victory-to-loss ratio of 19 to 1. With the arrival of the Hellcat in the fall of 1943, the air war in the Pacific favored the US Navy. The Hellcat was noted to be easy to fly and amazingly tough. Pilots joked that the brawny Hellcats seemed to contain melted-down steel from New York's Second Avenue elevated railway.

Joining the Hellcats in the fleet was a Grumman-designed torpedo bomber, nicknamed Avenger (ready to avenge the attack on Pearl Harbor). The big, three-man carrier plane could haul a 2,000-pound torpedo, and when most of Japan's navy was at the bottom of the Pacific, the plane could fly with an equal amount of conventional bombs to attack land-based targets.

Grumman's amphibious planes, named Duck, Goose, and Widgeon, served with the military as scout and transport aircraft in some of the most remote areas in the world during wartime.

As the war came to a close, Grumman was hard at work on a pair of newer fighters—one large machine and one small. The F7F Tigercat was a twin-engine fast fighter-bomber, while the diminutive F8F Bearcat was a powerful engine affixed to a pint-sized airframe. Neither saw combat, though the Bearcat came quite close when a handful of aircraft were deployed to the fleet before Japan's surrender.

Grumman built 17,428 planes from January 1940 to August 1945, representing 5.8 percent of the country's total output. At the height of employment, Grumman had about 25,500 men and women on its staff at factories in New York.

In order for Grumman to focus on fighters, versions of the simple and somewhat outdated J2F-6 Duck amphibious biplane were manufactured by Columbia Aircraft Corporation of Hempstead, New York. Grumman's Duck first flew in 1936. During wartime, the Navy, Marine Corps, and Coast Guard used the versatile machines for antisubmarine patrol duties, utility work, and air-sea rescue. (NA/USN.)

This image shows one of seven Grumman JRF-2 Goose amphibious flying boats operated by the US Coast Guard. Before the war, these aircraft were used for searching and mapmaking. After the United States entered the war, JRFs soldiered on—often loaded with bombs or depth charges, they cruised America's coastline looking for signs of enemy submarines. (NA/USN.)

When the next duty station was
more than 600 miles away, the
most efficient way to transport an
aircraft like the Goose was by ship.
Here, a Grumman JRF amphibian
is hoisted aboard the USS *Long
Island* (ACV-1) from a seaplane
wrecking derrick (YSD) off Palmyra
Island. This photograph was taken
on April 19, 1943. (NA/USN.)

A Grumman J4F Widgeon assigned
to patrol duties with the US Coast
Guard flies over the wreckage of
the USS *Lafayette* (AP-53) at Pier
88, New York City. The French
ocean liner SS *Normandie* was
seized by US authorities, and while
the vessel was being converted
to a troopship, it caught fire and
capsized in the Hudson River in
February 1942. On August 12, 1943,
salvage crews worked to right the
vessel, as shown here. (National
Museum of Naval Aviation.)

The original Wildcat design workups called for a traditional biplane. Brewster's Buffalo influenced a serious redesign. Hanging from the rafters in flight attitude for the benefit of press photographers, Grumman's new monoplane XF4F-2 debuted in 1937. Note the windows in the belly of the aircraft. Cutouts in the cockpit floor correspond to these openings to allow the pilot to see a target under the aircraft and help an aviator verify that the landing gear is down and locked before landing. (NA/USN.)

The Army Air Forces snapped what amounted to "mug shots" of many of the aircraft it evaluated at Wright Field. Photographs usually showed the subject aircraft from all angles, including head-on, from the side, and from directly overhead, as shown here. The perspective gives the viewer a look at the simple forms incorporated into the F4F for ease of production. As some pilots said, "The Wildcat had a barrel body and plank wings." (NA/USAAF.)

Gaggles of Grumman F4F-4 Wildcat fighters, with wings neatly folded, populate the hangar deck of the USS *Charger* (ACV-30). The aircraft carrier helped train Navy pilots for patrol and U-boat hunting operations in the North Atlantic. This picture, looking aft in the cramped storage compartment, was taken on October 2, 1942. (NA/USN.)

A pair of Grumman F4F-3A Wildcat fighters assigned to Fighter Squadron 2 (VF-2) cruise near Oahu in April 1942. What makes this photograph notable are the pilots. In the foreground, the F-1 is flown by Lt. Comdr. John S. Thach, the inventor of the Thach weave, a famous aerial combat tactic that allowed inferior US aircraft to defeat the Japanese Zero. Flying the F-13 is Lt. "Butch" O'Hare, the Navy's first ace. (NA/USN.)

Britain's Fleet Air Arm operated many Grumman-built fighters in combat. They called the F4F the Martlet. This image shows a pair of Martlets assigned to No. 881 Squadron shortly after a dusty landing at Royal Naval Air Station McKinnon Road in East Africa. Note the wing walkers dispatched to guide the aircraft though a swirl of dust kicked up by propellers. (NA/USN.)

Dirty, sunblasted, and exhausted, Marine technical sergeant R.W. Greenwood sits in the cockpit of an equally worn-down F4F-4 Wildcat on March 22, 1943. The battered fighter, based at Henderson Field on Guadalcanal and piloted by many different aviators, had taken part in 19 victories over Japanese aircraft. (NA/USN.)

Deck crews aboard the USS *Santee* (ACV-29) feed the .50-caliber guns of a F4F-4 Wildcat assigned to Escort Fighter Squadron 29 (VGF-29). A belt holding 240 rounds per gun could keep the F4F-4's six Browning M2s spitting lead for just 20 seconds. This picture is from November 1942, as the 14 planes of the squadron supported invasion operations in North Africa. (NA/USN.)

Headed east to support the invasion of North Africa, the USS *Ranger*'s (CV-4) complement of Grumman F4F-4 Wildcats are briefly parked sideways to allow for deck crews to test their .50-caliber machine guns. The noise, smoke, and distant splashes created quite a show, as evidenced by the number of sailors gathered behind the fighters. This photograph was taken from the *Ranger*'s island in early November 1942. (NA/USN.)

Ruby Reed and Merle Judd, labeled in the caption on this image as "aircraft production aides," work inside the cramped fuselage of a new Grumman fighter on the assembly line at Bethpage. Smaller than their male counterparts, "Rosies" were often assigned difficult jobs in small places—stringing wire harnesses, installing equipment, and holding a bucking bar for a riveter working on the exterior of the aircraft. (NA/USN.)

When General Motors took over Wildcat production, it allowed Grumman to focus on other vital projects. The later versions of the fighter, designated FM-2s, had a more powerful Wright-built engine and a taller tail to overcome the added torque. The fighters also had wing racks and could carry bombs or rockets. This FM-2 was photographed patrolling over the USS *Santee* (CVE-29) near the Philippines on October 20, 1944. (NA/USN.)

Zooming onto the scene behind a pair of 1,200-horsepower Wright Cyclone engines, the Grumman XF5F Skyrocket carrier-based interceptor first flew on April 1, 1940. The aircraft had many stellar traits, including counter-rotating propellers that made it stable during shipboard landings, exceptional visibility, and a more than satisfactory rate of climb. The catch was that twin-engine aircraft were complex, and the Navy settled on the simpler, more conventional F4F Wildcat. (NA/USN.)

Grumman also shopped a land-based version of the Skyrocket to the Army Air Corps in 1941. The new arrangement, designated the XP-50, eliminated the tail wheel in favor of a front wheel housed in an elongated nose. Other additions included self-sealing fuel tanks and armored panels for the pilot. Production versions were slated to fly with a pair of 20-mm cannon and a pair of machine guns, yet only one aircraft was made. The military judged other projects to be more important to the war effort. (NA/USAAF.)

The wings of most naval planes fold upward, which raises the plane's center of gravity and causes clearance issues on lower decks of an aircraft carrier. Leroy Grumman had the idea that wings should fold backward, just like a bird's wings. Grumman explained his plan to company engineers using a pink eraser with two paper clips stuck into it. His famous Sto-Wing design was used on the Wildcat, Hellcat, and the Avenger bomber, shown here aboard the USS *Santee* (CVE-29). (NA/USN.)

A Grumman TBF Avenger, its Twin Cyclone roaring, gets the signal to launch aboard an aircraft carrier. This photograph was taken by a member of famous photographer Edward Steichen's corps of cameramen, probably aboard the USS *Yorktown* (CV-10) in late 1942 or early 1943. (NA/USN.)

Grumman's TBF Avenger was built as a torpedo plane, its belly big enough to handle a single 161-inch-long Mark XIII aerial torpedo. Here, a crew prepares to load one of the 2,216-pound weapons into the aircraft. The plywood box around the missile's propeller and fins went with it. Designed to shatter upon contact with the water, the protective packaging assured that the weapon's critical components did not suffer dents or dings before combat. (NA/USN.)

A pair of Grumman Avengers cruise the coastline near Norfolk, Virginia, in December 1943. This view shows the lengthy bomb bay of the aircraft, which was built to hold an aerial torpedo that measures nearly 13.5 feet from end to end. Later, when most Japanese warships were gone, Avengers hefted up to a ton of general-purpose bombs. (NA/USN.)

Packed together as they make a hard turn near the target, TBM-3 Avengers of the escort carrier USS *Tulagi* (CVE-72) prepare to attack Japanese strongholds on Iwo Jima on March 2, 1945. When not involved in direct combat, the bombers switched to depth charges and flew antisubmarine patrols near the American invasion fleet. (NA/USN.)

In the cramped spaces of an escort carrier's deck, ordnance men deftly climb up to an Avenger's folded wings, reloading the bomber's .50-caliber wing guns. The light-colored paint scheme of white and gray indicates the planes were operating in the Atlantic, protecting Allied convoys from German U-boat attacks. Small escort carriers commonly operated with composite squadrons made up of New York–designed Grumman Wildcats and Avengers. (NA/USN.)

Not every moment overseas involved combat. Here, two members of a three-man aircrew participate in a famous military tradition of "hurry up and wait" at a remote airfield. The sheer size of the Avenger is evident when compared to the men. Though relaxed, they are ready to go on just a few minutes notice. The lounging aviator in the hammock is still wearing his life vest, goggles, helmet, and even his throat mic. (NA/USN.)

A TBM-3 from the USS *Bennington* (CV-20) pulls away from a bombing run over Chi Chi Jima with severe damage on February 18, 1945. Two crewmen bailed out and were later killed by Japanese fighters. The pilot, Ens. Robert King, stayed with the wounded aircraft, ditched near a destroyer, and survived the close call, later returning to flight duty. (NA/USN.)

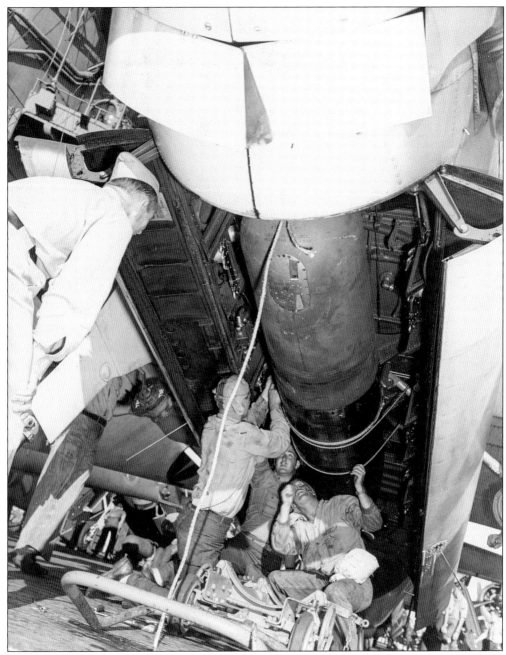

Aboard the USS *Lexington* (CV-16), crews load a heavy Mark XIII torpedo into the bomb bay of a Grumman TBF-1 Avenger torpedo bomber on September 12, 1943. The weapon's cradle can still be seen on the deck, and a hand-cranked winch marked "TBF" is at the ready on the right side of the aircraft. (NA/USN.)

So long, old friend. Stripped of useful parts, an Avenger from the USS *Sargent Bay* (CVE-83) gets a final catapult shot into the deep. The plane was severely damaged over Iwo Jima on February 25, 1945. The outer wing panels, engine, crew door, and other intact items were quickly wrenched free and would later be used to repair other aircraft. The deck crews punched hundreds of holes in the big bomber's skin to make sure it would sink moments after hitting the water. (NA/USN.)

This TBM took damage not from enemy action but from Mother Nature. Typhoon Louise hit Okinawa in October 1945. The Navy air base there lost 60 aircraft, including the small Piper NE-1 Cub liaison plane entangled in the sturdier and weightier Avenger. The bomber was evacuated to the island from the USS *Cape Gloucester* (CVE-109). (Author's collection.)

Over Okinawa, an Avenger assigned to Marine Torpedo Bomber Squadron 232 (VMTB-232) drops a pair of supply packs to troops below. Ropes, still attached to the aircraft, yank parachutes free once the cannisters have fallen away from the bomber. Famed Marine photographer David Douglas Duncan went along as part of the flight crew to capture this action with his camera. (NA/USMC.)

A young boy cannot believe his eyes. One moment he was walking along Cloverdale Street, and then an airplane fell from the sky on February 9, 1946. This TBM, based at Sand Point Naval Air Station near Seattle, lost power and attempted to make it to the runway at Boeing Field but only made it as far as Margaret Dillon's house in the South Park neighborhood. That year, she posted a claim for $5,612.84 for the total loss of her house. (NA/USN.)

Rolled out of the Bethpage factory for Grumman employees to see up close, the new prototype Hellcat, designated XF6F-1, was left bare to minimize weight and maximize performance during Navy testing. Several workers could not help but reach up to touch the smooth leading edges of this new Wilder Wildcat on January 6, 1942. (NA/USN.)

The prototype received a new R-2800 engine and an adjusted designation—XF6F-3. Grumman test pilot Bob Hall flew it with the new engine on July 30, 1942. A few weeks later, the Pratt & Whitney power plant went silent, and Hall had no choice but to bring the stricken fighter down for a crash landing in the fields of Crane's Farm on Long Island on August 17, 1942. Hall was hurt in the crash, and according to reports, the Hellcat was "moderately damaged." (NA/USN.)

Never known for its beautiful lines, the Hellcat was nevertheless a winner. Big and powerful, the fighter could better the Japanese Mitsubishi Zero in nearly every way. A young man who had never even seen an aircraft up close could learn to effectively fly and fight with the F6F in just a few months. The Navy touted the plane as "the first new American plane built out of combat experience in World War II." (NA/USN.)

During wartime, Grumman hired a trio of female test pilots: Elizabeth "Lib" Hooker (left), Cecil "Teddy" Kenyon (center), and Barbara Jayne (right). They spent their days wringing out new, top-of-the-line fighters and big torpedo bombers over Long Island Sound. Kenyon appeared in a Camel cigarette advertisement in 1944 with the tagline, "I Tame Hellcats!" (NA/USN.)

As the engine roars, a pair of young female plane captains make final adjustments to a Hellcat on the taxiway outside the Bethpage plant. At the time, the "Janes who made planes" (as they were called in a *Long Island Historical Journal* article) were about 30 percent of Grumman's workforce. The new fighters carried temporary abbreviated production numbers on their cowlings until they were reassigned to US Navy units operating in the Pacific. (NA/USN.)

As a Navy delegation tours the Grumman factory, strolling down a line of half-finished Hellcat fuselages, factory workers pause for a moment to say hello. After the fact, a military censor used his pen to designate items that should be painted out before the photograph hits the newspapers. Among the items destined to be hidden are the Hellcat's IFF (Identification Friend or Foe) antenna and production number placards, the latter of which could give an observer an idea of how many Hellcats had been built. (NA/USN.)

A Hellcat Mark I assigned to the Fleet Air Arm's No. 800 or No. 804 Squadron comes in for landing aboard the HMS *Emperor* in late 1944. The United Kingdom benefited greatly from lend-lease arrangements with the United States. The vessel in this photograph was built in Washington State, and the aircraft came off the assembly line at Grumman on Long Island. (NA/USN.)

A Hellcat reportedly flown by Navy ace "Butch" O'Hare was brought back to Long Island to serve as a testament to the strength of Grumman's products. This fighter, forged in Grumman's "Iron Works," gathered more than 200 bullet holes and still made it home. In this image, a Navy WAVE (Women Accepted for Volunteer Emergency Service) poses in the cockpit of the thoroughly sieved fighter plane. (NA/USN.)

The Hellcat's repertoire of weaponry included bombs and six heavy-hitting .50-caliber guns; in later models of the aircraft, it could carry HVARs (High Velocity Aerial Rockets). Here, deck crewmen prepare a stack of 3.5-inch rocket bodies affixed to a 5-inch naval shell nose in March 1945. Later versions of the rockets were produced with fatter 5-inch bodies for more range and velocity. (NA/USN.)

A landing signal officer (LSO) chooses to sprint to safety as an F6F-5 Hellcat pulls away after a fouled-up landing attempt. This picture was taken aboard the USS *Cabot* (CVL-28) off the Philippines in September 1944. A Grumman news publication notes that the fighter was able to use its roaring R-2800 engine to pull away from disaster and come around to try again. (NA/USN.)

A Grumman F6F-3 Hellcat from Navy Fighting Squadron Five (VF-5) pulls into position for launch aboard the USS *Yorktown* (CV-10) on November 20, 1943. Vapor trails swirl from the fighter's propeller tips as the pilot applies power. At the time, the aircraft were being sortied to targets in the Marshall Islands to cover US landings in the Gilbert Islands. (NA/USN.)

Fire erupts from a severed fuel line as Lt. (jg) A.W. Magee Jr. brings his Grumman F6F-3 Hellcat over the fantail for a landing aboard the USS *Cowpens* (CVL-25) on November 24, 1943. Photographed during combat operations over the Gilbert Islands, the Navy Fighting Squadron 25 (VF-25) aviator was unaware of the fire until he landed. The deck crew quickly extinguished the blaze, and Magee escaped by sprinting down the fighter's right wing and jumping to the flight deck. (NA/USN.)

His faithful Hellcat fighter in the background, Lt. (jg) Alexander Vraciu of Navy Fighting Squadron 16 (VF-16) is shown after he landed aboard the USS *Lexington* (CV-16). Vraciu grins as he holds up six gloved fingers, indicating the number of Japanese aircraft he shot down in eight minutes on June 19, 1944. The enemy planes were Yokosuka D4Y bombers (Allied code name Judy). Pilots later nicknamed the battle the Great Marianas Turkey Shoot. (NA/USN.)

Ens. Byron Johnson's F6F-3 Hellcat slid into the gun gallery of the USS *Enterprise* (CV-6) during a landing accident on November 10, 1943. The fighter's external fuel tank smashed, and a fire quickly erupted. In this image, catapult officer Lt. Walter Chewning is climbing onto the wing of the aircraft to pull Johnson from the wreck. The pilot survived the accident without serious injury. Chewning was awarded the Navy and Marine Corps Medal for his quick action. (NA/USN.)

The fight for Bougainville left a relic of the combat overhead. This F6F-3, named Good Deed Dotty, was hit over Augusta Bay and now lies in the silt at the mouth of the Piva River. The pilot was wounded in the action but later recovered. Here, a pair of Marines investigate the quickly deteriorating wreck on November 22, 1943. (NA/USMC.)

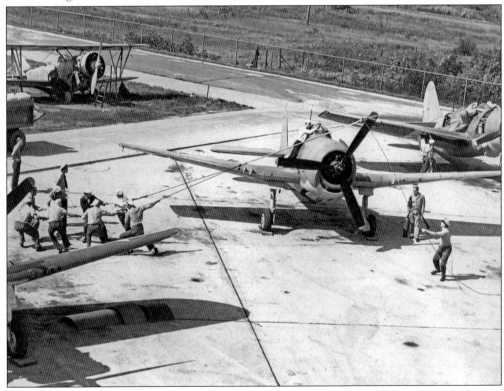

When an engine will not start on the deck of an aircraft carrier, the "dud" aircraft can foul up an intricate operation. Here, student sailors practice an alternate way to coax a Hellcat's Double Wasp to life. With a bungee rope, a crew of eight or more could prop start the big fighter. The angle was important to keep the ropes from getting swirled into the propeller. One sailor has a second line to drag the apparatus out of the way when the engine catches and chugs to life. (Author's collection.)

A new F6F-5 Hellcat gets a chance to be viewed by the masses during a war bond parade in New York City in early 1945. The wings were folded and the propeller was removed for the drive from Long Island, making the load nearly street legal. This picture was taken close to showtime, as the truck and display aircraft will slowly cruise down Fifth Avenue. (NA/USN.)

Going all-out to finance a global conflict meant getting the American public firmly on the side of war. This Hellcat was briefly the centerpiece of an exhibit on US Naval Aviation at Great Lakes Naval Training Station near Chicago in late 1944. As part of the sixth war loan campaign, extravagant displays like this one brought in recruits and funding. (National Archives New York City.)

Grumman's Tigercat prototype first flew in November 1943. With a pair of the same basic R-2800 engines that powered the Hellcat, the XF7F-1 was heavy and big, able to carry lots of weaponry. Despite its size, the new fighter was nearly 70 miles per hour faster than the Hellcat. Although it entered service too late for combat against the Japanese, versions of the Tigercat would fight during the Korean War. (NA/USN.)

Designed to zoom toward incoming kamikaze planes and quickly clobber them, the F8F Bearcat was an improved Hellcat hefting a ton less airframe into the skies. The first squadron of Bearcats was poised to fight in the Pacific as the war came to a close. In the crowded skies over Long Island Sound, Grumman aircraft were often emblazoned with the word "test" in an attempt to ward off local military pilots who rarely passed up a chance for a mock dogfight when a potential contender cruised nearby. (NA/USN.)

Five

REPUBLIC AVIATION CORPORATION

Republic rose from the ashes of the New York–based Seversky Aircraft Company in 1939. The name was chosen because Republic had the same number of letters as Seversky, which made it easy to quickly change the factory signage.

Russian-born aviator Alexander Seversky established his Farmingdale aircraft factory in 1931. Despite some early success with various aircraft designs, financial losses compelled the board of directors to oust Seversky from his own company. Republic went on, conceiving a handful of military machines for the US Army.

One of these aircraft became one of the most critical fighter planes of World War II for the United States. The P-47 Thunderbolt was born as an interceptor, used as a bomber escort, and then repurposed as a fighter-bomber; the latter is how the P-47 came to fame.

Lovingly called the Jug by pilots, the P-47 was brawny and big. The plane's hearty airframe and heavy complement of weaponry made it well-suited to hound German ground forces in Europe after the D-Day invasion. In the plane's fighter-bomber role, P-47 pilots took on the risky job of fighting enemy troops, trains, and tanks, clearing the way to Berlin for Allied forces.

Operating low to the ground often took its toll, yet the Thunderbolt was renowned for its ability to take punishment and return home. Pilots recall Jugs coming back absolutely mangled, dragging telephone lines or shredded tree branches pushed into smashed cowlings after a "too dangerous" low-level strafing run.

While the sleek California-designed P-51 Mustang gets a lot of the credit for winning the air war in Europe, New York's homely but effective P-47 was the workhorse of the conflict. The resilient Jug was more numerous and shot down more aircraft than the Mustang.

Near the end of the war, Republic began work on a jet fighter that was, in many ways, an updated P-47 with more modern propulsion. The first F-84 Thunderjet took to the skies in early 1946.

In another unusual wartime project, Republic collaborated with Ford to create copies of Germany's V-1 flying bomb. The American versions were designated Republic-Ford JB-1 Loons.

Republic built 15,603 planes from January 1940 to August 1945, representing 5.2 percent of the country's total wartime output. At the height of employment, Republic had about 25,000 men and women on its staff at factories in New York and Indiana.

A staple of the Army's prewar fighter force, along with Curtiss P-36s, was the Seversky P-35. These machines were assigned to the 1st Pursuit Group at Selfridge Field, Michigan, around 1938. The unit was the first air combat group formed by the American Expeditionary Force during World War I, and they carry the distinctive diving eagle insignia on their fuselage. (NA/USAAF.)

A look inside the cramped cockpit of a Seversky P-35 reveals a multitude of gauges and controls, with a main instrument panel and a secondary set of readouts for the fighter's Twin Wasp engine to the right. Note the embossed rudder pedals with the Seversky company logo. (NA/USAAF.)

An improved version of the P-35, the Seversky XP-41 incorporated a streamlined canopy, upgraded landing gear, and enhanced engine and supercharger components. Although the XP-41 was created concurrently with the P-43 Lancer project, the Army preferred the latter, and only one example of the XP-41 fighter was ever made. (NA/USAAF.)

As Seversky evolved to become Republic Aviation Corporation, improved versions of the P-35 flew for Army evaluators. While the XP-41 went by the wayside, the YP-43 (nicknamed Lancer) made the grade, at least for a while; 272 of the aircraft came from the Farmingdale factory in the years before the United States entered the war. However, air combat like the Battle of Britain made it clear that true wartime fighters would have to be much heartier and more sophisticated. (NA/USAAF.)

While Seversky P-43s were considered too outdated for the US Army to use in combat, the Chinese welcomed any type of combat plane they could pit against the Japanese. Here, American ferry command ground crewmen from Pennsylvania and Illinois pause to talk with a Chinese pilot on September 17, 1942. A little more than one third of all Lancers built went to China. (NA/USAAF.)

The XP-47B was a monster compared to Republic's other offerings of the era, powered by the same type of Pratt & Whitney R-2800 18-cylinder radial engine used in Vought's Corsair naval fighter. The P-47 Thunderbolt was, at the time, the largest and most expensive single-engine fighter in the Army's inventory. Note the swing-out side door used on the prototype aircraft. (NA/USAAF.)

The fuselage of Republic's P-47 was constructed in two halves. Top portions are shown in the foreground of this photograph taken at the Farmingdale plant on Long Island. In late October 1942, a second Republic plant in Evansville, Indiana, began making P-47s. And Curtiss, geared up for the P-60 contract that never materialized, began building P-47s under license at the end of 1942 in Buffalo. (NA/USAAF.)

At one point in 1944, Republic Aviation was putting out 28 new P-47s every day. The average was one every two hours. In this image, P-47Ds are near the end of the line at final assembly. Note the trolleys that run along slotted rails in the floor to help move each aircraft slowly forward. Near the end of the line, each new fighter gets pushed outside for fueling, final preparations, and test flights before delivery to the Army. (NA/USAAF.)

A banner implores New York's factory workers to "Keep That Line Rolling!" What is shown here is the culmination of weeks—and sometimes months—of work. Subcontractors at satellite facilities on Long Island, in New York City, and beyond created the hundreds of thousands of components that made up every Thunderbolt. As Henry Ford and his mass-production experts were fond of saying, "Don't let them get too big, too fast." Images like this show the cherry on top of the sundae—the last few hours before the new P-47s are fully finished. (NA/USAAF.)

On September 20, 1944, Republic's 10,000th P-47 Thunderbolt fighter rolled off the line at Farmingdale's plant. The *New York Times* described the day's event as "colorful ceremonies attended by thousands of workers, high ranking Army officials, and prominent civilians." The P-47D with serial number 44-20441 went on to serve with the 79th Fighter Group in Italy. The plane was lost in a midair collision over the Bay of Naples after the war. (NA/USAAF.)

Headed toward the front lines in Italy in 1944, a flight of 350th Fighter Group Thunderbolts carries a combined two tons of bombs on the wing pylons. The pair of aircraft in the middle are so new that they have not yet received their proper squadron markings. The aircraft in the foreground, a veteran, has made this run 100 times before, as indicated by the bomb tallies under its canopy. (NA/USAAF.)

At a base in Italy, ground crewmen work to exchange worn Pratt & Whitney Double Wasps for new ones in order to keep as many Thunderbolts as possible ready for the next mission. While it was a bit of a nightmare to work outside with minimal heavy equipment (or even firm, level ground), these engine swaps were set up to happen relatively quickly when compared to those of liquid-cooled engines of aircraft like the P-51 Mustang. (NA/USAAF.)

The first fighters sent overseas traveled in wooden crates. Over time, expediency and the sheer volume of aircraft needed in war zones drove change. Carefully sealed with tape and sheeting, this P-47 gets a spray-on protective coating before being loaded into a cargo vessel. Shielded from corrosive salt air and other hazards of shipboard life, the Thunderbolt would arrive in Europe or the Pacific in top shape, ready to be stripped down, washed, and then prepared for combat missions. (NA/USAAF.)

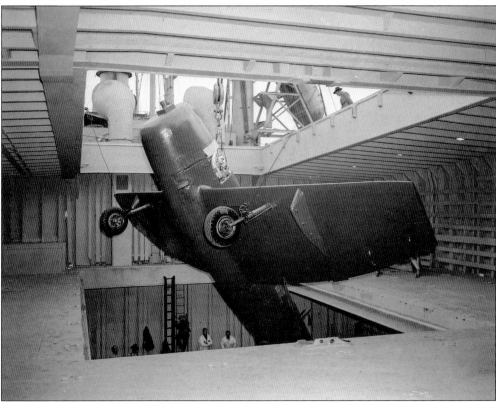

With its wingtips and propeller removed, a five-ton Thunderbolt is carefully lowered several decks into the hold of a Liberty ship bound for the Pacific. Once belowdecks, workmen carefully shift the big machines into parking places to maximize the cargo capacity. Other aircraft ride topside, perched over the top of decks and hatches. (National Archives Riverside.)

Another batch of new Thunderbolts arrives in Liverpool, England, in November 1943. Craned onto a lighter, the fighters move to shore. There, they are loaded onto specially modified trucks for a short drive to a local air base. Within days, they will be assigned to new units. (NA/USAAF.)

In November 1942, Operation Torch arrived in North Africa. Here, new fighters are brought ashore from cargo ships at Oran, Algeria. The original Army Air Forces caption says: "Like elephants in a circus parade, the P-47s are trundled through the North African port city to the airport, while native children and adults enjoy the show." (NA/USAAF.)

In a dogfight, the 56th Fighter Group's Lt. Justus Foster was singled out. His right wing was hit by five explosive 20-mm shells from a German fighter, and Foster skidded into a spin and lost his attackers. Back in England, he intentionally came in fast, because his ripped-apart flaps were nearly worthless. Though his Thunderbolt was shredded and battered, the lucky pilot survived without sustaining serious injury. (NA/USAAF.)

A P-47 pilot shows the bomber boys how it is done in the fall of 1943. Pressmen are lined up with their cameras to capture the scene. Flat-hatting, or flying low, was usually frowned upon because of the ever-present risk of a senseless accident. The Boeing B-17F Flying Fortress in the foreground, named Miss Patricia, was assigned to the 306th Bomb Group. The B-17 crashed during a takeoff accident on October 23, 1943, not long after this photograph was taken. (NA/USAAF.)

Maj. Walter Beckham, of the 353rd Fighter Group, had racked up 18 air-to-air victories when he posed for this photograph in February 1944. At the time, he was the highest-scoring American fighter pilot in Europe. A week later, his fighter, named Little Demon II, was hit by flak over Ostheim. Beckham spent the rest of the war as a POW and was liberated from a German camp in April 1945. (NA/USAAF.)

When the P-47 was being conceived, the lessons learned from the Battle of Britain in the summer of 1940 were still fresh on every designer's mind. Fighters of the future needed protection for the pilot and fuel tanks, and they needed heavy weaponry to make the most of that split second an enemy was in range. Engineers devised a way to compress the retracted main landing gear strut of the Thunderbolt in order to shoehorn in two more guns. In total, the P-47 carried eight .50-caliber guns, with four in each wing; six was the norm at the time. This sign is a warning to ground crews that the weaponry of this aircraft is loaded and ready to go. (NA/USAAF.)

These armorers are reloading some of the most successful guns in the European theater. Lt. Col. Francis "Gabby" Gabreski (not pictured), of the 56th Fighter Group, had already bagged many of his 28 wartime air-to-air victories when this photograph featuring his aircraft was taken in 1944. The open ammunition trays reveal the reason the guns of a P-47 are staggered, with one belt of bullets behind the next as they feed into the breach of each M2 machine gun. Gabreski's 166th combat mission was his last of World War II. On a strafing run on July 20, 1944, the propeller of his Thunderbolt touched the ground, and he was forced to crash-land behind enemy lines. He spent the rest of World War II as a prisoner of war in Stalag Luft I near Barth, Germany. (NA/USAAF.)

Lady Ruth, a P-47D assigned to the 318th Fighter Group, gets a quick turnaround at Aslito Airfield on Saipan. The Thunderbolt was launched from an escort carrier during the invasion of the island in June 1944. At the less than fully secured airfield, armorers load the guns while another crewman fills the fighter's 75-gallon external fuel tank. The pilot of the aircraft is standing on the opposite wing. (NA/USAAF.)

Days after the Normandy invasion, engineers built an airfield at Beuzeville, France, using wire matting. This P-47 ran into trouble when taking off on June 21, 1944, skidding to a stop and bursting into flames. Crewmen work to fight the fire before it reaches the wing pylons, which are packed with 20-pound AN-M1A1 antipersonnel bombs. (NA/USAAF.)

Pilots of the 353rd Fighter Group discuss the state of the world, ignoring the 500-pound general purpose bomb on the trolley at their feet. This picture was taken at an air base near Suffolk, England, on November 28, 1943. The aviators pictured hail from New Brunswick, New Jersey; St. Petersburg, Florida; and Richmond, Indiana. The noses of early-arriving P-47 Thunderbolts were often painted white and had white stripes on their tails so as not to be confused with German radial-engine Focke-Wulf Fw 190 fighters, which looked somewhat similar from a distance. (NA/USAAF.)

At an air base in Italy, ground crews of the 57th Fighter Group use a crane-equipped Cletrac tractor to lift the tail of a P-47D to flying attitude. They are working to boresight the fighter's machine guns and align the underwing triple M10 rocket tubes. Each tube fired a 4.5-inch projectile with roughly five pounds of explosive. (NA/USAAF.)

An oil line, ruptured by ground fire over Italy, left Lt. Edwin King with a problem. Though his R-2800 engine was still running, he could not see anything through his covered windscreen. As his engine temperature continued to rise and most of the 28 gallons of oil slathered aft and fell to earth, King managed to coax his wounded 350th Fighter Group Thunderbolt toward home by leaning out his open canopy. He flew in formation with another P-47 pilot to touch down safely on the runway at Pisa on January 12, 1945. (NA/USAAF.)

Strafing ground targets was hazardous business. This amazing image of a P-47 silhouetted against a massive explosion comes from a clip of gun camera footage. The 406th Fighter Group's Capt. Raymond Walsh and his wingman were shooting up German trucks near Normandy when one vehicle, carrying ammunition, violently erupted and threw up a curtain of debris and fire. Both fliers returned to base after the close call on June 23, 1944. (NA/USAAF.)

Decidedly too low on a strafing run, Lt. Richard Sulzbach's (left) Thunderbolt, aptly nicknamed Buzzin Cuzzin, crashed through a patch of trees in Italy but kept flying. The 350th Fighter Group pilot nursed the wounded fighter for 120 miles back to base with a crushed nose and ripped-up wings on April 1, 1945. Here, he and a fellow flier marvel at the pounding a Jug could take. (NA/USAAF.)

Some wiseacres might ask how many men it takes to refuel a P-47. Eight will do the trick for sure—with one being the pilot, Lt. Alfred Martin of Detroit, Michigan. At a forward base in Normandy, the 100-octane fuel flows from a GMC tanker truck to a 48th Fighter Group Thunderbolt while another, nicknamed Miss Lace, stands ready in the background. (NA/USAAF.)

After a mission to Berlin, a 78th Fighter Group Thunderbolt gets a freshly painted cowling of black and white checkers at Duxford, England. Distinctive colors and patterns were critical to fliers recognizing one another in the air. In both Europe and the Pacific, geometric shapes, letter codes, and bright hues helped announce affiliation without directly tipping off the enemy. (NA/USAAF.)

The P-47N was built for the vast distances of the Pacific. The internal fuel capacity of the N-model was 186 gallons more than previous models. The extra gas was stored in a pair of 93-gallon wing tanks located outboard of the guns and landing gear. The fighter's slightly longer wings were squared off at the wingtips and were hefty enough to carry three drop tanks—two 165-gallon and one 110-gallon—bringing the total fuel load to a whopping 1,266 gallons. (NA/USAAF.)

This deck full of P-47N Thunderbolts is heading to bases in the Pacific. This remarkable picture was taken on the USS *Casablanca* (CVE-55) in July 1945 while the carrier was en route to Guam. While production rates on most combat aircraft slowed in 1945, the number of Boeing B-29 bombers and long-range P-47N fighters stayed steady—or even increased—as US forces closed in on Japan. (NA/USAAF.)

Upon arrival at Ie Shima airfield off Okinawa, a pair of 318th Fighter Group ground crewmen make a new P-47N officially theirs by painting distinctive yellow and black stripes on the tail of the Thunderbolt. Much to the chagrin of many aircraft modelers, unit markings often went on fast and sloppy in order to quickly get the fighters into the skies. (NA/USAAF.)

When his sweetheart could not wait for him to return from the Central Pacific, Lt. "Herkie" Powell of the 414th Fighter Group got the dreaded letter from home. This sad turn of events necessitated a change in the nose art painted on the cowling of Powell's P-47N Thunderbolt while it was based on Iwo Jima. (7th FCA.)

While US pilots called the P-47 the Jug, a Mexican unit nicknamed the fighter *El Jarro*. Mexican and Brazilian pilots flew the Thunderbolt in combat in World War II. In this image, Mexican and US aircraft stand side by side at Clark Field in the Philippines. The one on the left is assigned to the 201 Escuadrón squadron. Looking closely, one can see the Mexican national insignia on the fighter's right wing and the vertical green, white, and red stripes on its rudder. (NA/USAAF.)

A crash landing "washed out" this 414th Fighter Group P-47N on Iwo Jima. Ground crews discarded the canopy and forward tail fairing to attach cables to the aircraft and lift it onto a flatbed truck. The plane would be stripped of useful parts and discarded, meaning that workers in New York would need to supply a replacement. (7th FCA.)

Test pilot Gerard DeMunck stands in front of a Curtiss Electric propeller with new hollow steel blades fitted to a Republic P-47 Thunderbolt. The cuffed blades, which pilots often called paddle props, had more surface area near the hub than the so-called toothpick blades used on the first P-47 models. This gave the Thunderbolt a small boost in performance and agility through more efficient use of horsepower. DeMunck joined Republic at Evansville in 1942 and later moved to Long Island, New York, to serve as an executive pilot into the 1960s. (NA/USAAF.)

The XP-47J was an attempt to enhance the Thunderbolt's performance. The lightened aircraft flew with six .50-caliber guns and a tight cowling around its R-2800 engine in November 1943. The Superbolt exceeded 500 miles per hour in test flights but was dropped for another Republic experimental fighter. The art on the nose is a depiction of Superman carrying a lance made of lightning. (NA/USAAF.)

Separate from all other Thunderbolt iterations was the XP-47H. Two P-47D airframes built in Indiana were stripped and modified to fly with a massive liquid-cooled Chrysler XIV-2220-1 inverted vee engine generating 2,300 horsepower. A long scoop situated under a long, bullet-shaped nose housed the radical power plant. Performance was less than expected, and the advent of jet engines curtailed any further development of the engine. (NA/USAAF.)

To kick off the fifth war loan drive on June 14, 1944, Republic set up an impressive exhibition in front of the J.P. Morgan and Company building on Wall Street. The centerpiece was a new P-47D Thunderbolt, complete with viewing platform. While it spent some time as the focal point of the financial district, it is unclear what happened to this particular aircraft after the event. (National Archives New York City.)

The aircraft sometimes referred to as the Ultrabolt was finished at Farmingdale on January 29, 1944. The XP-72 carried a 28-cylinder R-4360 Wasp Major engine that drove a massive 14-foot, 2-inch Curtiss Electric propeller. It was probably the largest diameter propeller fitted to a fighter and left only five inches of ground clearance, which meant takeoffs and landings required great care. Though the XP-72 was a great aircraft, the Army canceled the project in January 1945. (NA/USAAF.)

What happens to an airplane-building company with tons of tooling and floor space but vastly diminished military contracts? It diversifies. Former Republic employee Percival Spencer designed what would become the RC-3 Seabee amphibian, and Republic Aviation built over 1,000 of them in Farmingdale in 1946 and 1947. Most were made in the same factory that formerly produced Thunderbolts and would soon assemble thousands of F-84 Thunderjets. (NA/USAAF.)

Conceived in wartime, Republic's XF-12 Rainbow would "fly on all fours"—a company slogan highlighting that the reconnaissance aircraft had four engines, could go up to 40,000 feet, fly 4,000 miles, and reach 400 miles per hour. Made to photograph targets in Japan, the first of two streamlined speedsters took to the skies on February 4, 1946, well after V-J Day. By then, it was clear that jet-powered aircraft were the future. (NA/USAAF.)

Discover Thousands of Local History Books Featuring Millions of Vintage Images

Arcadia Publishing, the leading local history publisher in the United States, is committed to making history accessible and meaningful through publishing books that celebrate and preserve the heritage of America's people and places.

Find more books like this at
www.arcadiapublishing.com

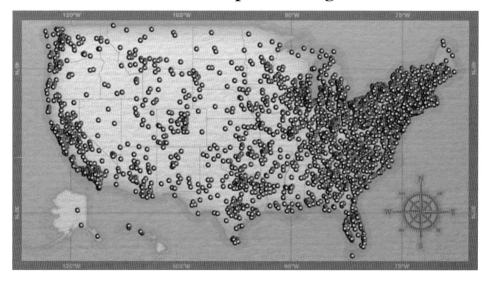

Search for your hometown history, your old stomping grounds, and even your favorite sports team.

Consistent with our mission to preserve history on a local level, this book was printed in South Carolina on American-made paper and manufactured entirely in the United States. Products carrying the accredited Forest Stewardship Council (FSC) label are printed on 100 percent FSC-certified paper.

MADE IN THE

USA